Old Kelso

John Griffiths

Kelso from the south bank of the River Tweed, extending from the grounds of Havannah House (Ednam House) at the right to the settlement of Wester Kelso on the left, dominated by Kelso Mill on the river's edge, and the spire of the North Kirk, to its left. The mill stands on the site of the Abbey Mill (a fragment of the medieval mill survives), and in 1901 was taken over by John Hogarth from A Dunn & Sons. Hogarth also ran Heiton and Maxwellheugh Mills, producing flour, oatmeal, pot and pearl barley. The company he founded still operates Kelso Mill, producing animal feed. The North Kirk was built 1865-67 as the Free Church, designed by the prolific Lincolnshire architect Frederick Pilkington. The incumbent minister (from 1837 to 1866) was the noted hymn-writer Dr Horatio Bonar, author of *I Heard the Voice of Jesus Say* and many other hymns. To the left, the River Teviot flows into the Tweed, with the wooded island, Kelso Anna, above the mill.

First published in the United Kingdom, 2010,
by Stenlake Publishing Ltd.
Telephone: 01290 551122
www.stenlake.co.uk

ISBN 9781840335071

Acknowledgements

The author is grateful to the staff of the Scottish Borders Archives at the Heritage Hub, Hawick, for their help, and to Mike Dyson of the National Traction Engine Trust for the traction engine information.

Bibliography

Kitty Cruft et al, *The Buildings of Scotland: Borders,* Yale University Press, London, 2006.
John Dent & Rory McDonald, *Farm and Factory: Revolution in the Borders,* Scottish Borders Council, Newtown St Boswells, 2001.
Alistair Moffat, *The Borders,* Deer Park Press, Selkirk, 2002.
Alistair Moffat, *Kelsae: A History of Kelso from Earliest Times,* Birlinn, 2006.
Jayne Shrimpton, *Family Photographs & How to Date Them,* Countryside Books, Newbury, 2008.

Left: Kelso's war memorial, on Bridge Street, was unveiled by the Duke of Roxburghe on Sunday 25th September 1921 in front of a crowd thought to number more than 4,000 and on a site, formerly occupied by the Abbey House, donated by him. The duke stands to the right of the column, the insignia of the Order of the Thistle prominent on his uniform, whilst to the left are the Rev D G Hamilton of Kelso Parish Church and the Rev T C Kirkwood of Trinity United Free Church. The officer between the two clergymen may be Lt. General Sir J M Babington of Pinnaclehill, the senior officer present. The monument was designed by Robert S Lorimer, who built many other memorials, including the National War Memorial at Edinburgh Castle, and it was constructed of white Northumberland sandstone. The bronze sculpture on the 34 feet high cross, depicting the triumph of good over evil, was by Charles d'Orville Pilkington Jackson. The names of the 243 townsmen killed in the First World War were recorded on bronze panels on the interior of the structure, one of which can be seen between the two clerics. A further panel was added after the Second World War.

Introduction

This book concentrates on a small area lying within a few miles radius of the historic town of Kelso, which is less than five miles from the border with England. This has done much to shape its history and that of the surrounding villages. Most of this area lay in the traditional county of Roxburghshire, but the parish of Nenthorn, between Stichill and Kelso, formed a promontory of Berwickshire territory.

Roxburgh was a castle town, dependent on its fortification, and in the thirteenth century, along with Edinburgh, Stirling and Berwick, one of Scotland's four royal burghs. It suffered greatly during the Anglo-Scottish wars, the fortress changing hands several times, and dwindled and disappeared altogether in the century or so after the final abandonment of the castle site. Blaeu's 1654 Atlas of Scotland, based on the late sixteenth century maps of Timothy Pont, indicates a church in an enclosure named *Freres*, on land south of the castle at the confluence of the Tweed and Teviot, presumably marking the Franciscan friary of St Peter, but there is no indication of the former town.

On the opposite side of the River Tweed the map shows the town of *Cailso*, clearly already a place of significance. Roy's Military Survey of 1747-55 shows Friars as merely two enclosures, without sign of habitation.

Kelso's name dates back to the Anglian period, deriving from Old English *Calc* 'chalk' *how* 'hill', referring to the ridge overlooking the Tweed on which the modern town stands. Its true genesis came in 1128, when King David re-established the monastery he had originally founded at Selkirk some fifteen years previously, and Kelso was recorded as an ecclesiastical burgh in 1237. It gradually came to supersede its military neighbour and prospered, despite damage by English incursions. The abbey suffered extensive damage, especially during the 'rough wooing' of 1545, when it was stormed by English troops and their Spanish mercenary allies and it suffered two major fires in the seventeenth century.

The Scottish Reformation, from 1525, and the Union of the Crowns in 1603 enabled Kelso's development to take a more peaceful route. The dissolution of Kelso Abbey in 1559 marked the end of the medieval economic overlords of the area, and much of its lands were acquired by the Kers of Cessford between 1576 and 1602. Sir Robert Ker became Lord Roxburghe in 1600, and in 1602 was formally granted the abbey estates, including the town of Kelso. In 1634 Kelso became a Burgh of Barony, rather than an ecclesiastical burgh. Lord Roxburghe was created Earl in 1616 and the fifth Earl, John Ker (1680-1741) was created Duke of Roxburghe in 1707. Under the patronage of the dukes, Kelso's population grew from perhaps 1,000 in the sixteenth century to 4,196 by the time of the first census in 1801, peaking at 5,192 in 1861. Around the time of many of the images in this book in the early twentieth century, the population numbered 3,982, but it had increased to 5,116 in 2001. The eighteenth century brought prosperity and expansion, with the establishment of the market place in the early part, the building of a bridge over the Tweed in 1755 (destroyed by floods in 1797 and replaced by the present bridge, designed by John Rennie, in 1801-04), and a new parish church in 1773. It gained a library in 1750, a public dispensary (Scotland's first) in 1777 and a newspaper (the *Kelso Mail*) in 1797. As the chief town of the district, it was at the centre of a network of turnpike roads constructed, or improved, in the course of the 18th century.

It maintained this prosperity throughout the 19th century, although it did not industrialise on a major scale. Unlike other Borders towns to the west, it was remote from the sheep-rearing uplands of western Roxburghshire, and on the slow, mature, Tweed rather than livelier rivers, it presented few attractions to woollen industry entrepreneurs. However, as railways replaced road traffic, the inns of Kelso were able to appeal to a relatively new type of traveller, the holiday maker anxious to experience the delights of 'Scott Country' or to cast for salmon in the Tweed or Teviot.

The surrounding countryside remained purely agricultural, rolling and fertile, studded with great houses in expansive grounds, but like the rest of Britain it was vulnerable to market forces. The great agricultural depression that began in the 1870s and lasted up to the First World War manifested itself in falling rural populations. Roxburghshire was no exception. Its population had reached a peak of 54,119 in 1861 then declined slowly to 53,741 in 1891, followed by a sharp drop to 48,804 in 1901 and 44,989 in 1921. This decline was matched by the villages in the agricultural north-east of the county covered in this volume.

However, the revival of road traffic in the twentieth century spared Kelso and the surrounding districts the worst excesses of the internal combustion engine. Rather than concentrating on Kelso as a busy service centre, as in the eighteenth century, the main north-south roads of the twentieth century (the A68, A697 and A1) passed at a distance to the west and east of the town, allowing Kelso to thrive without being strangled by traffic, and to display its charming and quiet urbanity.

Bridge Street, looking north towards the Square around 1900. The matching pilasters and balustrades on the shops on each side of the road (even though the buildings are of different designs and dates) show that some thought was given to providing a design unity to this important town gateway and the remodelling was carried out in 1872-73. The first shop on the left, with displays of photographs and postcards outside, is that of Alexander MacGregor. Two doors down (in 1906) are the grocers Halley and Co., and the first shop in the lower terrace of buildings is M & M Tait, newsagent. Beyond that terrace is the entrance to the grounds of Ednam House, now a hotel. Originally Havannah House, it was built in 1761 by James Nisbet as a house for James Dickson, an Ednam man who had fled the country after breaking the town pant (well) but became wealthy, working as a naval supplier. On the right, the first building bears the legend 'Family and Dispensing Chemist' and was run by A Gilchrist. Further along is the Spread Eagle Hotel, an early 19th century coaching inn. By 1906 its licensee was George A Combe and the hotel was registered with the Cyclists' Touring Club. It has since been converted into flats, with shops on the ground floor.

A later smilar photograph of Bridge Street shows a number of new developments. On the left, with its prominent gables is the Mock Tudor style Old Weigh House public house. Its name came from its proximity (by the entrance to Ednam House) to the town tron, or weigh-beam, where the measures of market traders were checked.

Town Hall, Kelso.   7249

Kelso Town Hall was built in 1816 to replace an earlier thatched tolbooth. The arches at street level were originally open, providing an arcade for market stalls, but in 1904-06 the openings were built up and the imposing main doorway, topped by the burgh arms, was added. The third building after the town hall on the left side of Woodmarket, rising above its neighbours, is the Border Temperance Hotel, run in the mid 1930s by Mrs Stempel. In 1906 it was run by James R Slight. The cloche hatted lady, crossing Woodmarket, dates the image to the late 1920s.

The Cross Keys Hotel, dominating Market Square, was built around 1760 by James Dickson of Ednam House, although the current frontage dates from 1879, when an additional storey was added. To the left of the hotel, in this early Edwardian photograph, is Forrest & Son, fishing tackle manufacturer, whilst to the right is the confectioner Wm Reid & Co.

2484.

THE SQUARE, KELSO.

This 1920s view shows the square already taking on its 20th century role as a car park, a matter of some controversy in the town. In 1921 Bailie Melrose succeeded in getting a committee to approve his plans to charge 'ordinary motors' one shilling and 'heavy cars and charabancs' two shillings to park in the square and side streets, but this was overturned by the town council, provoking furious argument in the letters column of the *Kelso Chronicle*. Kelso's growing popularity with day-trippers was helping to fuel traffic congestion in the town; the arrival of three charabancs filled with Musselburgh merchants and their families was just one of many such visits noted in the local press. The upper end of Horsemarket is seen to the left of the town hall, with the Black Swan prominent in the centre.

The Prince of Wales (later King Edward VIII) was in Kelso for the first time in 1926, as guest of the Duke of Roxburghe, to visit the Highland and Agricultural Society of Scotland Show at Springwood Park, one of seven occasions between 1832 and 1952 that the show was held at Kelso. Seen here on Friday 2nd July at the Market Place, the Prince was presented with an illustrated scroll by the Provost, Arthur Middlemass, and inspected a guard of honour comprising ex-servicemen. Behind the podium, John Anderson & Sons were drapers, and J M Massey was a pharmacist who had occupied the same premises since at least 1880. Next door, at number 18, were the premises of David Clow, furniture-maker, auctioneer and undertaker.

AFTER THE FAIR AT KELSO.

'After the Fair at Kelso', shows the Gypsy caravans which had come to Kelso for St James's Fair preparing to depart. The *Kelso Chronicle* of 11 August 1905 described such a post-fair scene: *By Sunday morning most of the shows and nomads had moved off, Kelso Square having for a time a lively appearance, and ere the afternoon the Fair ground had a rather deserted look.* The view is towards Bridge Street, and the building on the left is the Bank of Scotland, formerly the British Linen Company Bank, built in this form in 1885, and altered again in 1935 when its balcony was removed. The building on the far right, on the corner of Mill Wynd, with the projecting lantern, was the booksellers and publishers, J & J H Rutherfurd. James Hogarth Rutherfurd (1819-1903) had founded the company with his brother John, and published the *Southern Counties Record* and the annual *Borders Almanac*.

A crowd has gathered for the photographer who took this mid-Edwardian shot of Roxburgh Street. On the right are the premises of Thomas Johnston & Co, licensed grocer, and an advertisement for their 'Far Famed Special Blend' of whisky. Beyond are William Mercer's Temperance Hotel and William Rae the baker. On the left side is another licensed grocer, Robert Wright, the narrow entry of Duns Wynd, Andrew Liddle & Son, butchers, the Maybole Shoe and Boot shop run in 1906 by J Gray & Co, and at the end of the short terrace is the photographer and postcard publisher W H Stimpson who moved there around 1904, having previously occupied Liddle's premises. The gabled building beyond Stimpson's shop, built, according to its datestone, in 1897, was demolished and replaced by a supermarket in 1984. The view along the street is closed by the splendid spire of the North Kirk. Roxburgh Street is named in old documents as High Street, and led to the (now vanished) settlement of Wester Kelso, where there was a ferry across the Tweed to Roxburgh.

Horsemarket is one of the two main streets leading eastwards from Market Square. This image dates from 1923, with the solitary motor vehicle outnumbered by bicyclists and a milk float, and evidence of horse-drawn traffic in the middle of the road. On the left, Cullen & Murray advertise Fry's chocolate and next door is the Tweedside Motor Company, advertising Mobil and BP, as well as cars for hire. This building, with its imposing Venetian windows, and its further neighbour, have since been replaced by an uninspiring 1960s development. On the right is the Black Swan Hotel, whose licensee in 1935 was David Thomas. The building beyond the Black Swan has since been demolished and replaced by a concrete, single-storey, public convenience and a passageway to Woodmarket, useful amenities, but a poor contribution to the townscape.

A bazaar to raise funds for the construction of a cottage hospital at Kelso was opened on 12th October 1905 by Princess Christian of Schleswig-Holstein, born Princess Helena, the fifth child of Queen Victoria, and accompanied by her daughter, Princess Helena Victoria. The bazaar lasted a week and took place at the Corn Exchange which had been decorated to resemble a Venetian streetscape with *many rare and costly items* shown at the beautifully arranged stalls, which were run by eminent local families. The opening was overshadowed by the recent death of Lady Isobel Wilson (sister of the eighth Duke of Roxburghe), and at Princess Christian's request flags in the streets were taken down. The bazaar appears to have been a great success, raising almost £2,000 in the first two days. The platform party shown here comprises (standing left to right) Provost Crichton Smith, Lord Dunglass, the Earl of Dalkeith, Princess Christian, Princess Helena Victoria, C B Balfour of Newton Don, Major Wray (the princesses' equerry), the Earl of Haddington, Miss Emily Loch (lady in waiting), and Lady Nina Balfour.

Below: Designed by local architect James Nisbet, Kelso's octagonal parish church was built in 1771-73 on the old town butts (archery ground), replacing an older church which had made use of the nave of Kelso Abbey. The bellcote above the main (northern) entrance was added in 1823. This attractive building was not always admired. John Mason in 1826 described it as *a misshapen pile, bearing some resemblance to a mustard pot of immense size, and [it] pollutes the lovely scene amid which it stands*. A plan to rebuild the church had failed, so that *Kelso continues to be deformed by one of the least beautiful edifices that ever architecture reared*. Rutherfurd's Guide of 1880 was equally uncomplimentary, describing it as being *the ugliest and least suitable in its architecture of all the parish churches in Scotland - and that is saying a good deal, - but it is an excellent model for a circus.*

Right: Waverley Cottage, at the corner of Maxwell Street and The Butts, was built in the mid nineteenth century on the site of a house where Sir Walter Scott had stayed with his Aunt Jenny (Janet Scott) while attending Kelso Grammar School in 1783. He also stayed in Kelso, later in his youth, with his Uncle Robert of Rosebank House. Scott is commemorated by a bust in the centre of the gable wall, whilst over the doorway is a sculpture of Maida, his dog.

The town's pipe band in 1913, with two auxiliary drummer-boys!

KELSO R.U.F.C.

Rugby union is *the* team game of the Borders, and Kelso is no exception. Kelso RFC was founded in 1876 and this photo shows the team in the late 1930s. *Front row*: W Bookless, T Chalmers; *Middle row, left to right*: R Kennedy, D Bald, R Grieve (captain), A Anderson and J Bennett. *Back row*: A Smith, D Lindsay, A Gibb, J Campbell, J Blackadder, M Ballantyne, B Chalmers and H Aitchison.

Kelso High School in Edenside Road, and its knickerbockered pupils, in Edwardian days. In 1939 the new high school opened on Orchard Park, incorporating the public school which had been sited in the old grammar school on The Knowes. In 1905 the headmaster was John Kemp MA, and the teachers included Robert Rose (classics), G F Piggott (classics), W S Lawsie (mathematics), Miss Grant (modern languages), Alexander Goodfellow (science), James Wallace (art), A Tansley (violin, piano & organ), Miss Brown (piano), Mrs Adamson (preparatory department), Miss Anderson (cookery, domestic economy and needlework), C F Brown (shorthand) and T Bennie (manual instruction), while Sergeant Larken was the drill instructor. An advertisement in the *Kelso Chronicle* for the fee-paying school ran; *The school buildings are large and commodious, including excellent Laboratory, Music and Drawing Rooms, Workshop &c. … There is ample and excellent accommodation for boarders.*

The striking art deco Kelso High School on Bowmont Street, now a listed building, was built in 1936, to the designs of Reid & Forbes of Edinburgh, at a cost of £50,000. This view is now slightly obscured by later building, and the gate, gateposts and fencing, in the foreground, have been removed. Reid & Forbes did a good deal of work in the Borders, specialising in school buildings in the Modern Movement design, here with distinctive South American detailing.

Kelso from Teviot Road.

Maxwellheugh Mill in winter. It stands on a mill lade fed by the River Teviot and flowing into the Tweed just below the confluence of the two rivers. In 1852 it had been run by the Gledinning family and at the turn of the twentieth century by John Hogarth.

Kelso Station

A sign to the right of the young girl on the far platform, announcing that the North British Railway's new hotel at Waverley Station (now the Balmoral Hotel) is 'now open', dates this picture to 1902. The westbound train will have come from Berwick. The station was opened by the North British Railway in January 1851 (its line from St Boswells had opened on 17th January 1850 to a temporary terminus at Wallacenick, south of the town). The York, Newcastle & Berwick Railway (from 1854 part of the North Eastern Railway) had opened its Kelso branch as far as Sprouston in 1849, and through to Kelso on 1st June 1851. The NBR and NER lines converged at Mellendean, a mile to the north-east of Kelso Station. The branch closed to passenger services on 13th June 1964 and to freight on 1st April 1968 and the A698 Kelso bypass was built over the trackbed.

This picture, looking westwards, shows the station at a later date, indicated by the uniform of the railwayman and the lettering 'LNER' above a notice board. Formed in 1923, the London & North Eastern Railway incorporated both the North Eastern and North British Railways which had served Kelso.

The stone built, slate roofed, locomotive shed, built in 1851, to the east of Kelso Station. At its entrance were a turntable and a water column. In the 1930s, after this photograph was taken, one of the two tracks was lifted and although it was not used after 1955, it was not demolished until 1987.

4-4-2 tank engine, LNER number 9265, originally No. 265 of the North British Railway at Kelso Station. It was one of thirty locomotives, known as 'Yorkshire Tanks' or 'Yorkies', built between 1911 and 1913 by the Yorkshire Engine Company at Sheffield, designed by the NBR's locomotive superintendent William Paton Reid.

Springwood Park, standing at the confluence of Tweed and Teviot opposite Kelso, was built circa 1756 for Admiral James Douglas (1704-1787), who had bought the land in 1750 and changed its name from 'Bridgend'. The house was extensively rebuilt and enlarged 1850-53 by Brown & Wardrop, and at the time of this photograph, was the family home of Sir George Douglas, the fifth baronet, who had succeeded his father in 1885. An author and historian, he was steeped in the history, lore and legend, flora and fauna of the Borders, and among his many works was *A History of the Border Counties* (1897). Sir George had been born in Gibraltar and according to his obituary in *The Times, There was always a courtliness in the late baronet's habitual manner suggestive of the hidalgo*. He was succeeded by a spendthrift nephew, who bought a redundant destroyer after the Second World War to serve as a yacht and died in debt. Springwood Park was let, but fell into decay and was demolished in 1954. Chimney pieces from the house were installed in the modern house at Hendersyde. The annual Kelso ram sales, first held in 1836, moved to Springfield Park in 1943 and the Border Union Agricultural Show has been held here since 1946, when it replaced the old St James's Fair venue.

Maxwellheugh Cottages.

The cottages of Maxwellheugh Terrace, on Kelso's Station Road, are thought to have been built for Lady Scott-Douglas of Springwood Park in 1863, and present a picturesque scene with their red and cream sandstone, prominent gables, finials and barge boarding. While the cottages appear very northern European, almost Teutonic, their designer was from Gibraltar. Lady Scott-Douglas had been born Maria (or Mariquita) Juana Petronila de Pina, and married Sir George Scott-Douglas in 1851. The baronet died in 1885, but Lady Scott-Douglas survived until 1918, at the advanced age of 90 years.

A policeman and curious onlookers stand by the wreckage of a traction engine involved in *an extraordinary and even frightful accident* at around 7.00 am on Saturday, 30th March 1907. The engine, owned by the Kelso District Committee of Roxburgh County Council, had been hauling two wagons filled with road material down the bank from Kelso Railway Station towards the bridge, when the weight of the load and *the sudden springing of a pin in an important part of the mechanism* led Driver Hay to lose control. In attempting to negotiate the sharp corner onto the Jedburgh road, where the uphill gradient might have brought it to a halt, he smashed into the garden wall and bank of the Abbey Temperance Hotel. No blame attached to Hay, recorded the *Kelso Chronicle*, *a steady, faithful servant of the county authorities for over 23 years*, although it neglected to record whether or not he had been injured.

Manufactured by Aveling and Porter of Rochester, Kent, it had an 8 horse power, single cylinder, engine and was delivered to the Kelso District Committee of the county roads department in 1896. It was returned to Aveling and Porter in 1910, perhaps as a 'trade in', and was still in use elsewhere as late as 1932.

Kelso Cottage Hospital, on Jedburgh Road, was built in 1906-07 to the designs of Sydney Mitchell & Wilson, a prolific Edinburgh-based architectural practice, and is shown here recently-opened in this image of 1907. It closed in 1993.

Inchmyre Rifle Range Opening Ceremony — A.M.

The Duchess of Roxburghe officiating at the opening of the Kelso miniature rifle range on Inch Myre, near the Tweed, east of the town, in a field provided by the tenant, Mr Rutherford. Note the (presumably red) flag, and the rifle, fixed in a vice to provide a 'bulls-eye' inaugural shot. The miniature rifle movement, inspired by Field Marshal Lord Roberts, hoped to promote marksmanship amongst young men in case of international crisis, and was embraced enthusiastically in Roxburghshire. Kelso Rifle Club was founded at a public meeting at the Corn Exchange on 30th July 1906, chaired by Provost Crichton Smith, and within a few weeks membership (at a subscription of half-a-crown) was approaching one hundred. The first recorded match was in November, and the official opening took place sometime in late 1906 or early 1907. The club president, Sir Richard Waldie-Griffith of Hendersyde, is presumably among those present.

Left: This elderly gentleman was *the veteran of the district*, according to an inscription on the back of the photograph dated, Kelso, 1910. *He had a nasty fall the other week, but there has been no bad effects and the bruises are healing quickly.*

Roxburgh Street & Entrance to Floors Castle, Kelso.   A.2313.

Above: Roxburgh Street runs westward from the Market Place to the gates of Floors Castle. The gates, piers and gatehouses date from 1928-29 and were designed by Reginald Fairlie, designer of the Dukes of Roxburghe Memorial Cloister at Kelso Abbey (1933), and the National Library of Scotland in Edinburgh. The lodges, with their 'bellcast' roofs, bear carved heraldic badges. To the left is a unicorn's head and the motto, *Pro Christo et Patria Dulce Periculum* (For Christ and country, danger is sweet) of the Ker family and to the right, a boar's head, with the motto *Be Traist* (Be true), of the Innes family (the family name of the dukes being Innes-Ker). The ducal arms are displayed on the ironwork above the gates. The walls of the park around the castle were built 1810-14 by French prisoners of war.

27

The exterior of Floors Castle, designed 1837-47 by W H Playfair in a Renaissance-Jacobean style for the sixth Duke of Roxburghe, hides an earlier core. Part of this older building had been designed by William Adams in the 1720s; part was a conversion of an older tower house (giving Floors a fig-leaf of legitimacy in describing itself as a castle). This eighteenth century building has been described as *severely plain, not to say heavy looking*, a far cry from Playfair's concoction. Floors had come into the hands of the Ker family of Cessford after the dissolution of Kelso Abbey and the sale of its lands, and has remained the family seat. The Earldom of Roxburghe was created in 1616, and the fifth earl was created a duke in 1707.

02539. DINING ROOM, FLOORS CASTLE, KELSO. Poulton.

The State Dining Room at Floors Castle, in the early twentieth century, with its geometric ceiling and ornamental woodwork. Looking westwards, it offers beautiful views over the Tweed Valley and the Cheviot Hills. The master of Floors at this time was Henry Innes-Ker, the 8th Duke of Roxburghe (1876-1932), who succeeded to the title in 1892. Like many British aristocrats of the period, he married (in 1903) an American heiress, Mary Goelet, who brought a dowry of $20 million.

Winston Churchill, a cousin of the Duke of Roxburghe, speaking at the great garden fete held by the Roxburgh and Selkirk Unionist Association at Floors Castle on 3rd September 1927, when he was Chancellor of the Exchequer. Special trains brought Unionist (Conservative) activists to Kelso, and 1,100 vehicles converged on the park. The platform party included the Duke and Duchess of Roxburghe, former Prime Minister Earl Balfour, Mrs Churchill, the Earl of Dalkeith (the local Unionist candidate) and others, while Field Marshal Earl Haig was also present. Churchill, on his first visit to the Borders, spoke optimistically on the state of the economy, public spending, the state of agriculture, and British policy on disarmament. The microphone, apparently floating in front of Churchill, was suspended by wire from the platform woodwork, having been rigged up by Pollock Brothers of Jedburgh.

Makerstoun House, a mile south of the eponymous village, stands on the north bank of the Tweed. It is built around a house constructed to replace one destroyed during Hertford's 'rough wooing' in 1545, and which was incorporated into a building of 1725 designed by William Adam. This was greatly embellished in 1812 by Archibald Elliot to produce the version of Makerstoun shown in this late 1930s view. However, following a fire in 1970 the 19th century additions were removed and the house rebuilt to Adams' plans. In the mid 19th century Makerstoun belonged to Sir Thomas and Lady Makdougall Brisbane. Sir Thomas, a former governor of New South Wales after whom the Australian city was named, was keenly interested in astronomy and built the world's first magnetic astronomical observatory in the park at Makerstoun. In April 1920 the house, with 2,500 acres and some of the best salmon fishing on the Tweed, was sold by Hugh Scott-Makdougall to James Bell-Irving for £105,000. Bell-Irving, who died in 1936, was a retired *Taipan*: he had been head of Jardine Mathieson and a member of the Hong Kong Legislative and Executive Councils.

MANOR HILL COTTAGES,

Model cottages in the hamlet of Makerstoun, part of the estate owned by the Scott-Makdougall family of Makerstoun House, around 1912.

Part of the village of Old Nenthorn, on the banks of the Eden Water north-west of Kelso. There had been a medieval settlement here, and up to the late 18th century there was a settlement by the parish church. The population of the parish peaked at 461 in 1861, but by 1901, shortly before this photograph was taken, had fallen to 416. By 1981 it had declined, again, to 117.

Nenthorn House was built in 1894 to the designs of George Beattie & Son, at a cost of £20,000. It was the heart of a 1,875 acre estate, which in 1910, some ten years after this photograph, was sold to a Manchester businessman, M J F Ferreira, for £50,000.

Also on the Nenthorn estate, a short distance from the late Victorian mansion, is Old Nenthorn House. It probably incorporates part of an earlier building, but was rebuilt in the late 18th century, with an east wing (the part of the building to the left of the picture) added around fifty years later. This served as the 'big house' of the estate until the modern Nenthorn House was built in 1894. Old Nenthorn House lost its roof in the late 1940s.

Newton Don, in Nenthorn parish, was built 1817-20 for Sir Alexander Don. The Dons owned the estate from the late 17th century until it was sold to Charles Balfour in 1847. The architect was Robert Smirke, who also designed the British Museum; the *porte cochere* (carriage porch) was added in 1860. John Mason in 1826 described the house as superb and its gardens *in exquisite taste … In the midst of them is a fine canal, on which swans float gracefully, and bend their necks of pride to behold their image reflected in the liquid mirror*. At the time of this photograph, Newton Don was owned by Captain Charles Barrington Balfour and his wife Lady Helena ('Nina'), pillars of Borders society. Captain Balfour succeeded his father at the age of ten. He served in the army (including the Egyptian campaign of 1882), and stood several times for Parliament in the Borders, before being elected MP for Hornsey in 1900 (when he was unopposed). He resigned his seat in 1907 and from 1917 until his death he was Lord Lieutenant of Berwickshire. He also sat on Berwickshire County Council, and was chairman of Nenthorn Parish Council and the school board. The house served as a hospital during both World Wars.

This scene of Stichill Village, north of Kelso on the road to Greenlaw, is remarkably similar today, although the tree on the left has gone and Rosemount Cottage, to its left, is no longer a police station. The topographical writer Francis Groome commented that Stichill *occupies a beautiful site* but *has greatly decayed since the close of the 18th century, when it was famous for the open-air preaching, or 'holy fairs' of the Secession Church*. Rutherfurd's *Kelso Past & Present: A Guide* (1880) noted that *some new cottages are about to be erected* and these are probably the row shown here.

Stitchell House in 1897, when owned by the Forfarshire born brewer James Deuchar. The 60,000 acre estate dates from 1124 and was owned by the Gordons until 1628 when it was sold to the Pringles. They held it until 1855 when it was bought by the Bairds who, in 1895, sold it to Deuchar. The house pictured here was designed by James Maitland Wardrop of Edinburgh in 1866. He specialised in judicial buildings and prisons until an advantageous marriage (Anna Maria, fifth daughter of James Dundas, 24th and last of Dundas) introduced him to the landed gentry and commissions such as Stitchell (a variant of the name Stichill). In 1931 the house, and 73 acres, was advertised for sale at the 'scrap price' of £2,500, *suitable for a hotel, institution or holiday home*, but it was demolished in 1938, leaving some outbuildings.

Ednam takes its name from the Eden Water, *a pretty little place, of hoar antiquity* according to Francis H Groome's *Ordnance Gazetteer of Scotland*. This Edwardian image shows proud cottagers posing for the camera, though perhaps not so proud as to remove the washing, airing on the hedges. In 1851, Ednam parish had a population of 658, but a century later this had fallen to 412, and by 1981 to just 203, a typical story for rural places in the Borders.

Hendersyde House, overlooking the Tweed north of Kelso, was built in 1802-03 for George Waldie, extended circa 1840, and demolished to build a new house in 1938-40. At the time of this 1915 photograph it was home to Sir Richard Waldie-Griffith, a sporting baronet, whose wealth derived from coal and lignite mines in Bohemia. Sir Richard had a reputation as a fine amateur oarsman, but was best known on the turf, maintaining a large stud at Hendersyde, coming third in the table of winners in 1899. He was also a noted collector of art, mosaics and classical antiquities. In 1904 he bought the Ednam estate from the Earl of Dudley, becoming Laird of Ednam.

Gipsy participants at St James' Fair on Tweedside Haugh, or Fairgreen, opposite Floors Castle, probably, in the 1930s. According to a 1905 account, *Gipsy encampments, always a source of interest to the visitor, stretched from the entrance to the fair and Show ground … right along to the Roxburgh Castle entrance*. The fair dated from the twelfth century and had 'belonged' to the Royal Burgh of Roxburgh. After that town disappeared its prerogatives devolved to the nearest Royal Burgh, Jedburgh, and so it was the Provost of Jedburgh who traditionally proclaimed the fair each year on August 5th (or 6th, if the 5th was a Sunday). There was a great trade in horses and ponies by Gipsy dealers, known as 'muggers', perhaps a corruption of 'Magyar'. By the 1930s it was in decline and did not survive the War, being succeeded by the Border Union Agricultural Show at Springwood Park.

Roxburgh Castle stood on a narrow headland between the rivers Tweed and Teviot, overlooking Kelso and the lost town of Roxburgh (distinct from the modern Roxburgh village, two miles to the south). Little remains of this major fortification, first built in the twelfth century, held periodically under English control, destroyed by the Scots in 1314, reoccupied and rebuilt by the English King Edward III after 1334, and only recaptured by the Scots in 1460, when the explosion of a cannon at the siege of Roxburgh cost the life of the Scots King, James II. It was demolished again by the Scots after its recapture, but reoccupied and rebuilt as an artillery fort by the English in 1547. The castle was handed back to the Scots in 1551 and promptly dismantled again, this time for good. With the castle died the town of Roxburgh, a Royal Burgh and once one of the main urban centres in Scotland with four churches: St John's which was within the castle walls, St James, Holy Sepulchre, and the Franciscan Friary of St Peter . No physical trace of any of these remains.

The village of Roxburgh, two miles south of the Royal Burgh of Roxburgh. This panoramic view shows many of the village buildings, although it omits the two most significant structures namely the stone railway viaduct of 1850, which carried the St Boswells-Kelso railway across the River Teviot, and the remains of Wallace's Tower, a border fortification modified after its destruction by English invaders in 1545. At the far left is the late Victorian schoolhouse and to its right the parish church of 1752, greatly extended in 1878. It probably stands on the site of an older church. The other buildings in the picture show a stark contrast between the traditional single-storey cottages in the centre and the improved dwellings which possibly are post-World War One 'homes for heroes' at the right hand side. Many were thatched, a practice which only died out in the 1950s along with the district's last thatcher. The population of Roxburgh was 1,178 in 1861 but by 1951 had almost halved, to 602.

Heiton

Heiton, part of the parish of Roxburgh, lies south of Kelso on the A698 road to Hawick and Jedburgh. Much of the village is owned by the Merchant Company of Edinburgh. These mid-Victorian cottages on Main Street show elaborate bargeboard detailing around the eaves and windows, and elaborate glazing, some of which survives.

Heiton Mill on the banks of the Teviot, two miles south of Kelso. At the time of this photograph, around 1915, it was in the possession of Robert Hogarth who died in 1939 and whose family also ran Kelso Mill.

Sunlaws House, as shown in this Edwardian image, dates largely from 1885-86, when it was rebuilt after a fire, to the designs of John Watherston & Sons. The estate had been acquired by the Kerr family in 1600, and Sunlaws House developed from an 18th century building, which was enlarged on several occasions. It was substantially extended by David Rhind in 1835-43 for William Scott-Kerr, but damaged in a fire in 1885. When this picture was taken, it was the home of Robert Scott-Kerr (1859-1942), a veteran of the Zulu, South African and First World Wars, who rose to the rank of brigadier. In the 1960s the estate was bought by the Duke of Roxburghe and the house used as an estate office. In 1982 it was converted into a country house hotel, now called the Roxburghe Hotel. It looks much as in this photograph, except that the tower has lost its spirelets and its cloak of ivy.

Wooden House lies on the south bank of the Tweed just downstream of Kelso. In 1852 it is recorded as being occupied by Colonel Duncan Gordon Scott and Captain George Scott, RN and in 1880, as the residence of J Addison Scott. In 1906, not long after this photograph was taken, it was a residence of Charles John Cunningham, who died the same year at his home Muirhouselaw, Maxton. Cunningham was described in his obituary as *one of the best all-round sportsmen in the Border country*, who had taken part several times in the Grand National, and he was also a Deputy Lieutenant of Roxburghshire.

LEMPITLAW. UPPER ROW

Lempitlaw is a farming hamlet three miles east of Kelso, two miles from the English border. The cottages in the foreground still stand, albeit extensively remodeled.

This magnificent engine and its crew worked for Roxburgh County Council Roads Department, Melrose District Committee, and is a single cylinder B6 road locomotive. Built by John Fowler & Co of Leeds around 1928, it was delivered in June 1933, and given the registration number KS 5863. In 1940 it was sold to Moorhead & Son of Stirling, and in 1953 was in the possession of J & A White of Aberdour. The County Roads Committee must have been one of the most blue-blooded committees in Scottish local government; in 1925 it included two dukes (Buccleuch and Roxburghe) and the Earl of Ellesmere.